State of the Union Addresses of James Madison

James Madison

Works of the Public Domain

TABLE OF CONTENTS

November 29, 1809

December 5, 1810

November 5, 1811

November 4, 1812

December 7, 1813

September 20, 1814

December 5, 1815

December 3, 1816

State of the Union Address
James Madison
November 29, 1809
Fellow-Citizens of the Senate and House of Representatives:

At the period of our last meeting I had the satisfaction of communicating an adjustment with one of the principal belligerent nations, highly important in itself, and still more so as presaging a more extended accommodation. It is with deep concern I am now to inform you that the favorable prospect has been over-clouded by a refusal of the British Government to abide by the act of its minister plenipotentiary, and by its ensuing policy toward the United States as seen through the communications of the minister sent to replace him.

Whatever pleas may be urged for a disavowal of engagements formed by diplomatic functionaries in cases where by the terms of the engagements a mutual ratification is reserved, or where notice at the time may have been given of a departure from instructions, or in extraordinary cases essentially violating the principles of equity, a disavowal could not have been apprehended in a case where no such notice or violation existed, where no such ratification was reserved, and more especially where, as is now in proof, an engagement to be executed without any such ratification was contemplated by the instructions given, and where it had with good faith been carried into immediate execution on the part of the United States.

These considerations not having restrained the British Government from disavowing the arrangement by virtue of which its orders in council were to be revoked, and the event authorizing the renewal of commercial intercourse having thus not taken place, it necessarily became a question of equal urgency and importance whether the act prohibiting that intercourse was not to be considered as remaining in legal force. This question being, after due deliberation, determined in the affirmative, a proclamation to that effect was issued. It could not but happen, however, that a return to this state of things from that which had followed an execution of the arrangement by the United States would involve difficulties. With a view to diminish these as much as possible, the instructions from the Secretary of the Treasury now laid before you were transmitted to the collectors of the several ports. If in permitting British vessels to depart without giving bonds not to proceed to their own ports it should appear that the tenor of legal authority has not been strictly pursued, it is to be ascribed to the anxious desire which was felt that no individuals should be injured by so unforeseen an occurrence; and I rely on the regard of Congress for the equitable interests of our own citizens to adopt whatever further provisions may be found requisite for a general remission of penalties involuntarily incurred.

The recall of the disavowed minister having been followed by the appointment of a successor, hopes were indulged that the new mission would contribute to alleviate the disappointment which had been produced, and to remove the causes which had so long embarrassed the good understanding of the two nations. It could not be doubted that it would at least be charged with conciliatory explanations of the step which had been taken and with proposals to be substituted for the rejected arrangement.

Reasonable and universal as this expectation was, it also has not been fulfilled. From the first official disclosures of the new minister it was found that he had received no authority to enter into explanations relative to either branch of the arrangement disavowed nor any authority to substitute proposals as to that branch which concerned the British orders in council, and, finally, that his proposals with regard to the other branch, the attack on the frigate Chesapeake, were founded on a presumption repeatedly declared to be inadmissible by the United States, that the first step toward adjustment was due from them, the proposals at the same time omitting even a reference to the officer answerable for the murderous aggression, and asserting a claim not less contrary to the British laws and British practice than to the principles and obligations of the United States.

The correspondence between the Department of State and this minister will show how unessentially the features presented in its commencement have been varied in its progress. It will show also that, forgetting the respect due to all governments, he did not refrain from imputations on this, which required that no further communications should be received from him. The necessity of this step will be made known to His Britannic Majesty through the minister plenipotentiary of the United States in London; and it would indicate a want of the confidence due to a Government which so well understands and exacts what becomes foreign ministers near it not to infer that the misconduct of its own representative will be viewed in the same light in which it has been regarded here. The British Government will learn at the same time that a ready attention will be given to communications through any channel which may be substituted. It will be happy if the change in this respect should be accompanied by a favorable revision of the unfriendly policy which has been so long pursued toward the United States.

With France, the other belligerent, whose trespasses on our commercial rights have long been the subject of our just remonstrances, the posture of our relations does not correspond with the measures taken on the part of the United States to effect a favorable change. The result of the several communications made to her Government, in pursuance of the authorities vested by Congress in the Executive, is contained in the correspondence of our minister at Paris now laid before you.

By some of the other belligerents, although professing just and amicable dispositions, injuries materially affecting our commerce have not been duly controlled or repressed. In these cases the interpositions deemed proper on our part have not been omitted. But it well deserves the consideration of the Legislature how far both the safety and the honor of the American flag may be consulted, by adequate provisions against that collusive prostitution of it by individuals unworthy of the American name which has so much flavored the real or pretended suspicions under which the honest commerce of their fellow citizens has suffered.

In relation to the powers on the coast of Barbary, nothing has occurred which is not of a nature rather to inspire confidence than distrust as to the continuance of the existing amity. With our Indian neighbors, the just and benevolent system continued toward them has also preserved peace, and is more and more advancing habits favorable to their civilization and happiness.

From a statement which will be made by the Secretary of War it will be seen that the fortifications on our maritime frontier are in many of the ports completed, affording the defense which was contemplated, and that a further time will be required to render complete the works in the harbor of New York and in some other places. By the enlargement of the works and the employment of a greater number of hands at the public armories the supply of small arms of an improving quality appears to be annually increasing at a rate that, with those made on private contract, may be expected to go far toward providing for the public exigency.

The act of Congress providing for the equipment of our vessels of war having been fully carried into execution, I refer to the statement of the Secretary of the Navy for the information which may be proper on that subject. To that statement is added a view of the transfers of appropriations authorized by the act of the session preceding the last and of the grounds on which the transfers were made.

Whatever may be the course of your deliberations on the subject of our military establishments, I should fail in my duty in not recommending to your serious attention the importance of giving to our militia, the great bulwark of our security and resource of our power, an organization best adapted to eventual situations for which the United States ought to be prepared.

The sums which had been previously accumulated in the Treasury, together with the receipts during the year ending on the 30th of September last (and amounting to more than $9 millions), have enabled us to fulfill all our engagements and to defray the current expenses of Government without recurring to any loan. But the insecurity of our commerce and the consequent diminution of the public revenue will probably produce a deficiency in the receipts of the ensuing year, for which and for other details I refer to the statements which will be transmitted from the Treasury.

In the state which has been presented of our affairs with the great parties to a disastrous and protracted war, carried on in a mode equally injurious and unjust to the United States as a neutral nation, the wisdom of the National Legislature will be again summoned to the important decision on the alternatives before them. That these will be met in a spirit worthy the councils of a nation conscious both of its rectitude and of its rights, and careful as well of its honor as of its peace, I have an entire confidence; and that the result will be stamped by a unanimity becoming the occasion, and be supported by every portion of our citizens with a patriotism enlightened and invigorated by experience, ought as little to be doubted.

In the midst of the wrongs and vexations experienced from external causes there is much room for congratulation on the prosperity and happiness flowing from our situation at home. The blessing of health has never been more universal. The fruits of the seasons, though in particular articles and districts short of their usual redundancy, are more than sufficient for our wants and our comforts. The face of our country ever presents evidence of laudable enterprise, of extensive capital, and of durable improvement. In a cultivation of the materials and the extension of useful manufactures, more especially in the general application to household fabrics, we behold a rapid diminution of our dependence on foreign supplies. Nor is it unworthy of reflection that this revolution in our pursuits and habits is in no slight degree a consequence of those impolitic and arbitrary edicts by which the contending nations, in endeavoring each of them to obstruct our trade with the other, have so far abridged our means of procuring the productions and manufactures of which our own are now taking the place.

Recollecting always that for every advantage which may contribute to distinguish our lot from that to which others are doomed by the unhappy spirit of the times we are indebted to that Divine Providence whose goodness has been so remarkably extended to this rising nation, it becomes us to cherish a devout gratitude, and to implore from the same omnipotent source a blessing on the consultations and measures about to be undertaken for the welfare of our beloved country.

***

State of the Union Address
James Madison
December 5, 1810
Fellow-Citizens of the Senate and House of Representatives:

The embarrassments which have prevailed in our foreign relations, and so much employed the deliberations of Congress, make it a primary duty in meeting you to communicate whatever may have occurred in that branch of our national affairs.

The act of the last session of Congress concerning the commercial intercourse between the United States and Great Britain and France and their dependencies having invited in a new form a termination of their edicts against our neutral commerce, copies of the act were immediately forwarded to our ministers at London and Paris, with a view that its object might be within the early attention of the French and British Governments.

By the communication received through our minister at Paris it appeared that knowledge of the act by the French Government was followed by a declaration that the Berlin and Milan decrees were revoked, and would cease to have effect on the first day of November ensuing. These being the only known edicts of France within the description of the act, and the revocation of them being such that they ceased at that date to violate our neutral commerce, the fact, as prescribed by law, was announced by a proclamation bearing date the 2nd of November.

It would have well accorded with the conciliatory views indicated by this proceeding on the part of France to have extended them to all the grounds of just complaint which now remain unadjusted with the United States. It was particularly anticipated that, as a further evidence of just dispositions toward them, restoration would have been immediately made of the property of our citizens under a misapplication of the principle of reprisals combined with a misconstruction of a law of the United States. This expectation has not been fulfilled.

From the British Government no communication on the subject of the act has been received. To a communication from our minister at London of a revocation by the French Government of its Berlin and Milan decrees it was answered that the British system would be relinquished as soon as the repeal of the French decrees should have actually taken effect and the commerce of neutral nations have been restored to the condition in which it stood previously to the promulgation of those decrees. This pledge, although it does not necessarily import, does not exclude the intention of relinquishing, along with the others in council, the practice of those novel blockades which have a like effect of interrupting our neutral commerce, and this further justice to the United States is the rather to be looked for, in as much as the blockades in question, being not more contrary to the established law of nations than inconsistent with the rules of blockade formally recognized by Great Britain herself, could have no alleged basis other than the plea of retaliation alleged as the basis of the orders in council.

Under the modification of the original orders of November, 1807, into the orders of April, 1809, there is, indeed, scarcely a nominal distinction between the orders and the blockades. One of those illegitimate blockades, bearing date in May, 1806, having been expressly avowed to be still unrescinded, and to be in effect comprehended in the orders in council, was too distinctly brought within the purview of the act of Congress not to be comprehended in the explanation of the requisites to a compliance with it. The British Government was accordingly apprised by our minister near it that such was the light in which the subject was to be regarded.

On the other important subjects depending between the United States and the Government no progress has been made from which an early and satisfactory result can be relied on.

In this new posture of our relations with those powers the consideration of Congress will be properly turned to a removal of doubts which may occur in the exposition and of difficulties in the execution of the act above cited.

The commerce of the United States with the north of Europe, heretofore much vexed by licentious cruisers, particularly under the Danish flag, has latterly been visited with fresh and extensive depredations. The measures pursued in behalf of our injured citizens not having obtained justice for them, a further and more formal interposition with the Danish Government is contemplated. The principles which have been maintained by that Government in relation to neutral commerce, and the friendly professions of His Danish Majesty toward the United States, are valuable pledges in favor of a successful issue.

Among the events growing out of the state of the Spanish Monarchy, our attention was imperiously attracted to the change developing itself in that portion of West Florida which, though of right appertaining to the United States, had remained in the possession of Spain awaiting the result of negotiations for its actual delivery to them. The Spanish authority was subverted and a situation produced exposing the country to ulterior events which might essentially affect the rights and welfare of the Union. In such a conjuncture I did not delay the interposition required for the occupancy of the territory west of the river Perdido, to which the title of the United States extends, and to which the laws provided for the Territory of Orleans are applicable. With this view, the proclamation of which a copy is laid before you was confided to the governor of that Territory to be carried into effect. The legality and necessity of the course pursued assure me of the favorable light in which it will present itself to the Legislature, and of the promptitude with which they will supply whatever provisions may be due to the essential rights and equitable interests of the people thus brought into the bosom of the American family.

Our amity with the powers of Barbary, with the exception of a recent occurrence at Tunis, of which an explanation is just received, appears to have been uninterrupted and to have become more firmly established.

With the Indian tribes also the peace and friendship of the United States are found to be so eligible that the general disposition to preserve both continues to gain strength.

I feel particular satisfaction in remarking that an interior view of our country presents us with grateful proofs of its substantial and increasing prosperity. To a thriving agriculture and the improvements related to it is added a highly interesting extension of useful manufactures, the combined product of professional occupations and of household industry. Such indeed is the experience of economy as well as of policy in these substitutes for supplies heretofore obtained by foreign commerce that in a national view the change is justly regarded as of itself more than a recompense for those privations and losses resulting from foreign injustice which furnished the general impulse required for its accomplishment. How far it may be expedient to guard the infancy of this improvement in the distribution of labor by regulations of the commercial tariff is a subject which can not fail to suggest itself to your patriotic reflections.

It will rest with the consideration of Congress also whether a provident as well as fair encouragement would not be given to our navigation by such regulations as would place it on a level of competition with foreign vessels, particularly in transporting the important and bulky productions of our own soil. The failure of equality and reciprocity in the existing regulations on this subject operates in our ports as a premium to foreign competitors, and the inconvenience must increase as these may be multiplied under more favorable circumstances by the more than countervailing encouragements now given them by the laws of their respective countries.

Whilst it is universally admitted that a well-instructed people alone can be permanently a free people, and whilst it is evident that the means of diffusing and improving useful knowledge form so small a proportion of the expenditures for national purposes, I can not presume it to be unseasonable to invite your attention to the advantages of superadding to the means of education provided by the several States a seminary of learning instituted by the National Legislature within the limits of their exclusive jurisdiction, the expense of which might be defrayed or reimbursed out of the vacant grounds which have accrued to the nation within those limits.

Such an institution, though local in its legal character, would be universal in its beneficial effects. By enlightening the opinions, by expanding the patriotism, and by assimilating the principles, the sentiments, and the manners of those who might resort to this temple of science, to be redistributed in due time through every part of the community, sources of jealousy and prejudice would be diminished, the features of national character would be multiplied, and greater extent given to social harmony. But, above all, a well-constituted seminary in the center of the nation is recommended by the consideration that the additional instruction emanating from it would contribute not less to strengthen the foundations than to adorn the structure of our free and happy system of government.

Among the commercial abuses still committed under the American flag, and leaving in force my former reference to that subject, it appears that American citizens are instrumental in carrying on a traffic in enslaved Africans, equally in violation of the laws of humanity and in defiance of those of their own country. The same just and benevolent motives which produced interdiction in force against this criminal conduct will doubtless be felt by Congress in devising further means of suppressing the evil.

In the midst of uncertainties necessarily connected with the great interests of the United States, prudence requires a continuance of our defensive and precautionary arrangement. The Secretary of War and Secretary of the Navy will submit the statements and estimates which may aid Congress in their ensuing provisions for the land and naval forces. The statements of the latter will include a view of the transfers of appropriations in the naval expenditures and in the grounds on which they were made.

The fortifications for the defense of our maritime frontier have been prosecuted according to the plan laid down in 1808. The works, with some exceptions, are completed and furnished with ordnance. Those for the security of the city of New York, though far advanced toward completion, will require a further time and appropriation. This is the case with a few others, either not completed or in need of repairs.

The improvements in quality and quantity made in the manufacture of cannon and small arms, both at the public armories and private factories, warrant additional confidence in the competency of these resources for supplying the public exigencies.

These preparations for arming the militia having thus far provided for one of the objects contemplated by the power vested in Congress with respect to that great bulwark of the public safety, it is for their consideration whether further provisions are not requisite for the other contemplated objects of organization and discipline. To give to this great mass of physical and moral force the efficiency which it merits, and is capable of receiving, it is indispensable that they should be instructed and practiced in the rules by which they are to be governed. Toward an accomplishment of this important work I recommend for the consideration of Congress the expediency of instituting a system which shall in the first instance call into the field at the public expense and for a given time certain portions of the commissioned and non-commissioned officers. The instruction and discipline thus acquired would gradually diffuse through the entire body of the militia that practical knowledge and promptitude for active service which are the great ends to be pursued. Experience has left no doubt either of the necessity or of the efficacy of competent military skill in those portions of an army in fitting it for the final duties which it may have to perform.

The Corps of Engineers, with the Military Academy, are entitled to the early attention of Congress. The buildings at the seat fixed by law for the present Academy are so far in decay as not to afford the necessary accommodation. But a revision of the law is recommended, principally with a view to a more enlarged cultivation and diffusion of the advantages of such institutions, by providing professorships for all the necessary branches of military instruction, and by the establishment of an additional academy at the seat of Government or elsewhere. The means by which war, as well for defense as for offense, are now carried on render these schools of the more scientific operations an indispensable part of every adequate system.

Even among nations whose large standing armies and frequent wars afford every other opportunity of instruction these establishments are found to be indispensable for the due attainment of the branches of military science which require a regular course of study and experiment. In a government happily without the other opportunities seminaries where the elementary principles of the art of war can be taught without actual war, and without the expense of extensive and standing armies, have the precious advantage of uniting an essential preparation against external danger with a scrupulous regard to internal safety. In no other way, probably, can a provision of equal efficacy for the public defense be made at so little expense or more consistently with the public liberty.

The receipts into the Treasury during the year ending on the 30th of September last (and amounting to more than $8.5 millions) have exceeded the current expenses of the Government, including the interest on the public debt. For the purpose of reimbursing at the end of the year $3.75 millions of the principal, a loan, as authorized by law, had been negotiated to that amount, but has since been reduced to $2.75 millions, the reduction being permitted by the state of the Treasury, in which there will be a balance remaining at the end of the year estimated at $2 millions. For the probable receipts of the next year and other details I refer to statements which will be transmitted from the Treasury, and which will enable you to judge what further provisions may be necessary for the ensuing years.

Reserving for future occasions in the course of the session whatever other communications may claim your attention, I close the present by expressing my reliance, under the blessing of Divine Providence, on the judgement and patriotism which will guide your measures at a period particularly calling for united councils and flexible exertions for the welfare of our country, and by assuring you of the fidelity and alacrity with which my cooperation will be afforded.

***

State of the Union Address
James Madison
November 5, 1811
Fellow-Citizens of the Senate and House of Representatives:

In calling you together sooner than a separation from your homes would otherwise have been required I yielded to considerations drawn from the posture of our foreign affairs, and in fixing the present for the time of your meeting regard was had to the probability of further developments of the policy of the belligerent powers toward this country which might the more unite the national councils in the measures to be pursued.

At the close of the last session of Congress it was hoped that the successive confirmations of the extinction of the French decrees, so far as they violated our neutral commerce, would have induced the Government of Great Britain to repeal its orders in council, and thereby authorize a removal of the existing obstructions to her commerce with the United States.

Instead of this reasonable step toward satisfaction and friendship between the two nations, the orders were, at a moment when least to have been expected, put into more rigorous execution; and it was communicated through the British envoy just arrived that whilst the revocation of the edicts of France, as officially made known to the British Government, was denied to have taken place, it was an indispensable condition of the repeal of the British orders that commerce should be restored to a footing that would admit the productions and manufactures of Great Britain, when owned by neutrals, into markets shut against them by her enemy, the United States being given to understand that in the mean time a continuance of their nonimportation act would lead to measures of retaliation.

At a later date it has indeed appeared that a communication to the British Government of fresh evidence of the repeal of the French decrees against our neutral trade was followed by an intimation that it had been transmitted to the British plenipotentiary here in order that it might receive full consideration in the depending discussions. This communication appears not to have been received; but the transmission of it hither, instead of founding on it an actual repeal of the orders or assurances that the repeal would ensue, will not permit us to rely on any effective change in the British cabinet. To be ready to meet with cordiality satisfactory proofs of such a change, and to proceed in the mean time in adapting our measures to the views which have been disclosed through that minister will best consult our whole duty.

In the unfriendly spirit of those disclosures indemnity and redress for other wrongs have continued to be withheld, and our coasts and the mouths of our harbors have again witnessed scenes not less derogatory to the dearest of our national rights than vexation to the regular course of our trade.

Among the occurrences produced by the conduct of British ships of war hovering on our coasts was an encounter between one of them and the American frigate commanded by Captain Rodgers, rendered unavoidable on the part of the latter by a fire commenced without cause by the former, whose commander is therefore alone chargeable with the blood unfortunately shed in maintaining the honor of the American flag. The proceedings of a court of inquiry requested by Captain Rodgers are communicated, together with the correspondence relating to the occurrence, between the Secretary of State and His Britannic Majesty's envoy. To these are added the several correspondences which have passed on the subject of the British orders in council, and to both the correspondence relating to the Floridas, in which Congress will be made acquainted with the interposition which the Government of Great Britain has thought proper to make against the proceeding of the United States.

The justice and fairness which have been evinced on the part of the United States toward France, both before and since the revocation of her decrees, authorized an expectation that her Government would have followed up that measure by all such others as were due to our reasonable claims, as well as dictated by its amicable professions. No proof, however, is yet given of an intention to repair the other wrongs done to the United States, and particularly to restore the great amount of American property seized and condemned under edicts which, though not affecting our neutral relations, and therefore not entering into questions between the United States and other belligerents, were nevertheless founded in such unjust principles that the reparation ought to have been prompt and ample.

In addition to this and other demands of strict right on that nation, the United States have much reason to be dissatisfied with the rigorous and unexpected restrictions to which their trade with the French dominions has been subjected, and which, if not discontinued, will require at least corresponding restrictions on importations from France into the United States.

On all those subjects our minister plenipotentiary lately sent to Paris has carried with him the necessary instructions, the result of which will be communicated to you, by ascertaining the ulterior policy of the French Government toward the United States, will enable you to adapt to it that of the United States toward France.

Our other foreign relations remain without unfavorable changes. With Russia they are on the best footing of friendship. The ports of Sweden have afforded proofs of friendly dispositions toward our commerce in the councils of that nation also, and the information from our special minister to Denmark shews that the mission had been attended with valuable effects to our citizens, whose property had been so extensively violated and endangered by cruisers under the Danish flag.

Under the ominous indications which commanded attention it became a duty to exert the means committed to the executive department in providing for the general security. The works of defense on our maritime frontier have accordingly been prosecuted with an activity leaving little to be added for the completion of the most important ones, and, as particularly suited for cooperation in emergencies, a portion of the gun boats have in particular harbors been ordered into use. The ships of war before in commission, with the addition of a frigate, have been chiefly employed as a cruising guard to the rights of our coast, and such a disposition has been made of our land forces as was thought to promise the services most appropriate and important.

In this disposition is included a force consisting of regulars and militia, embodied in the Indiana Territory and marched toward our northwestern frontier. This measure was made requisite by several murders and depredations committed by Indians, but more especially by the menacing preparations and aspect of a combination of them on the Wabash, under the influence and direction of a fanatic of the Shawanese tribe. With these exceptions the Indian tribes retain their peaceable dispositions toward us, and their usual pursuits.

I must now add that the period is arrived which claims from the legislative guardians of the national rights a system of more ample provisions for maintaining them. Notwithstanding the scrupulous justice, the protracted moderation, and the multiplied efforts on the part of the United States to substitute for the accumulating dangers to the peace of the two countries all the mutual advantages of reestablished friendship and confidence, we have seen that the British cabinet perseveres not only in withholding a remedy for other wrongs, so long and so loudly calling for it, but in the execution, brought home to the threshold of our territory, of measures which under existing circumstances have the character as well as the effect of war on our lawful commerce.

With this evidence of hostile inflexibility in trampling on rights which no independent nation can relinquish, Congress will feel the duty of putting the United States into an armor and an attitude demanded by the crisis, and corresponding with the national spirit and expectations.

I recommend, accordingly, that adequate provisions be made for filling the ranks and prolonging the enlistments of the regular troops; for an auxiliary force to be engaged for a more limited term; for the acceptance of volunteer corps, whose patriotic ardor may court a participation in urgent services; for detachments as they may be wanted of other portions of the militia, and for such a preparation of the great body as will proportion its usefulness to its intrinsic capacities. Nor can the occasion fail to remind you of the importance of those military seminaries which in every event will form a valuable and frugal part of our military establishment.

The manufacture of cannon and small arms has proceeded with due success, and the stock and resources of all the necessary munitions are adequate to emergencies. It will not be inexpedient, however, for Congress to authorize an enlargement of them.

Your attention will of course be drawn to such provisions on the subject of our naval force as may be required for the services to which it may be best adapted. I submit to Congress the seasonableness also of an authority to augment the stock of such materials as are imperishable in their nature, or may not at once be attainable.

In contemplating the scenes which distinguish this momentous epoch, and estimating their claims to our attention, it is impossible to overlook those developing themselves among the great communities which occupy the southern portion of our own hemisphere and extend into our neighborhood. An enlarged philanthropy and an enlightened forecast concur in imposing on the national councils an obligation to take a deep interest in their destinies, to cherish reciprocal sentiments of good will, to regard the progress of events, and not to be unprepared for whatever order of things may be ultimately established.

Under another aspect of our situation the early attention of Congress will be due to the expediency of further guards against evasions and infractions of our commercial laws. The practice of smuggling, which is odious everywhere, and particularly criminal in free governments, where, the laws being made by all for the good of all, a fraud is committed on every individual as well as on the state, attains its utmost guilt when it blends with a pursuit of ignominious gain a treacherous subserviency, in the transgressors, to a foreign policy adverse to that of their own country. It is then that the virtuous indignation of the public should be enabled to manifest itself through the regular animadversions of the most competent laws.

To secure greater respect to our mercantile flag, and to the honest interests which it covers, it is expedient also that it be made punishable in our citizens to accept licenses from foreign governments for a trade unlawfully interdicted by them to other American citizens, or to trade under false colors or papers of any sort.

A prohibition is equally called for against the acceptance by our citizens of special licenses to be used in a trade with the United States, and against the admission into particular ports of the United States of vessels from foreign countries authorized to trade with particular ports only.

Although other subjects will press more immediately on your deliberations, a portion of them can not but be well bestowed on the just and sound policy of securing to our manufactures the success they have attained, and are still attaining, in some degree, under the impulse of causes not permanent, and to our navigation, the fair extent of which is at present abridged by the unequal regulations of foreign governments.

Besides the reasonableness of saving our manufactures from sacrifices which a change of circumstances might bring on them, the national interest requires that, with regard to such articles at least as belong to our defense and our primary wants, we should not be left in unnecessary dependence on external supplies. And whilst foreign governments adhere to the existing discriminations in their ports against our navigation, and an equality or lesser discrimination is enjoyed by their navigation in our ports, the effect can not be mistaken, because it has been seriously felt by our shipping interests; and in proportion as this takes place the advantages of an independent conveyance of our products to foreign markets and of a growing body of mariners trained by their occupations for the service of their country in times of danger must be diminished.

The receipts into the Treasury during the year ending on the 30th day of September last have exceeded $13.5 millions, and have enabled us to defray the current expenses, including the interest on the public debt, and to reimburse more than $5 millions of the principal without recurring to the loan authorized by the act of the last session. The temporary loan obtained in the latter end of the year 1810 has also been reimbursed, and is not included in that amount.

The decrease of revenue arising from the situation of our commerce, and the extraordinary expenses which have and may become necessary, must be taken into view in making commensurate provisions for the ensuing year; and I recommend to your consideration the propriety of insuring a sufficiency of annual revenue at least to defray the ordinary expenses of Government, and to pay the interest on the public debt, including that on new loans which may be authorized.

I can not close this communication without expressing my deep sense of the crisis in which you are assembled, my confidence in a wise and honorable result to your deliberations, and assurances of the faithful zeal with which my cooperating duties will be discharged, invoking at the same time the blessing of Heaven on our beloved country and on all the means that may be employed in vindicating its rights and advancing its welfare.

***

State of the Union Address
James Madison
November 4, 1812
Fellow-Citizens of the Senate and House of Representatives:

On our present meeting it is my first duty to invite your attention to the providential favors which our country has experienced in the unusual degree of health dispensed to its inhabitants, and in the rich abundance with which the earth has rewarded the labors bestowed on it. In the successful cultivation of other branches of industry, and in the progress of general improvement favorable to the national prosperity, there is just occasion also for our mutual congratulations and thankfulness.

With these blessings are necessarily mingled the pressures and vicissitudes incident to the state of war into which the United States have been forced by the perseverance of a foreign power in its system of injustice and aggression.

Previous to its declaration it was deemed proper, as a measure of precaution and forecast, that a considerable force should be placed in the Michigan Territory with a general view to its security, and, in the event of war, to such operations in the uppermost Canada as would intercept the hostile influence of Great Britain over the savages, obtain the command of the lake on which that part of Canada borders, and maintain cooperating relations with such forces as might be most conveniently employed against other parts.

Brigadier-General Hull was charged with this provisional service, having under his command a body of troops composed of regulars and of volunteers from the State of Ohio. Having reached his destination after his knowledge of the war, and possessing discretionary authority to act offensively, he passed into the neighboring territory of the enemy with a prospect of easy and victorious progress. The expedition, nevertheless, terminated unfortunately, not only in a retreat to the town and fort of Detroit, but in the surrender of both and of the gallant corps commanded by that officer. The causes of this painful reverse will be investigated by a military tribunal.

A distinguishing feature in the operations which preceded and followed this adverse event is the use made by the enemy of the merciless savages under their influence. Whilst the benevolent policy of the United States invariably recommended peace and promoted civilization among that wretched portion of the human race, and was making exertions to dissuade them from taking either side in the war, the enemy has not scrupled to call to his aid their ruthless ferocity, armed with the horrors of those instruments of carnage and torture which are known to spare neither age nor sex. In this outrage against the laws of honorable war and against the feelings sacred to humanity the British commanders can not resort to a plea of retaliation, for it is committed in the face of our example. They can not mitigate it by calling it a self-defense against men in arms, for it embraces the most shocking butcheries of defenseless families. Nor can it be pretended that they are not answerable for the atrocities perpetrated, since the savages are employed with a knowledge, and even with menaces, that their fury could not be controlled. Such is the spectacle which the deputed authorities of a nation boasting its religion and morality have not been restrained from presenting to an enlightened age.

The misfortune at Detroit was not, however, without a consoling effect. It was followed by signal proofs that the national spirit rises according to the pressure on it. The loss of an important post and of the brave men surrendered with it inspired everywhere new ardor and determination. In the States and districts least remote it was no sooner known than every citizen was ready to fly with his arms at once to protect his brethren against the blood-thirsty savages let loose by the enemy on an extensive frontier, and to convert a partial calamity into a source of invigorated efforts. This patriotic zeal, which it was necessary rather to limit than excite, has embodied an ample force from the States of Kentucky and Ohio and from parts of Pennsylvania and Virginia. It is placed, with the addition of a few regulars, under the command of Brigadier-General Harrison, who possesses the entire confidence of his fellow soldiers, among whom are citizens, some of them volunteers in the ranks, not less distinguished by their political stations than by their personal merits. The greater portion of this force is proceeding in relieving an important frontier post, and in several incidental operations against hostile tribes of savages, rendered indispensable by the subserviency into which they had been seduced by the enemy--a seduction the more cruel as it could not fail to impose a necessity of precautionary severities against those who yielded to it.

At a recent date an attack was made on a post of the enemy near Niagara by a detachment of the regular and other forces under the command of Major-General Van Rensselaer, of the militia of the State of New York. The attack, it appears, was ordered in compliance with the ardor of the troops, who executed it with distinguished gallantry, and were for a time victorious; but not receiving the expected support, they were compelled to yield to reenforcements of British regulars and savages. Our loss has been considerable, and is deeply to be lamented. That of the enemy, less ascertained, will be the more felt, as it includes among the killed the commanding general, who was also the governor of the Province, and was sustained by veteran troops from unexperienced soldiers, who must daily improve in the duties of the field.

Our expectation of gaining the command of the Lakes by the invasion of Canada from Detroit having been disappointed, measures were instantly taken to provide on them a naval force superior to that of the enemy. From the talents and activity of the officer charged with this object everything that can be done may be expected. Should the present season not admit of complete success, the progress made will insure for the next a naval ascendancy where it is essential to our permanent peace with and control over the savages.

Among the incidents to the measures of the war I am constrained to advert to the refusal of the governors of Maine and Connecticut to furnish the required detachments of militia toward the defense of the maritime frontier. The refusal was founded on a novel and unfortunate exposition of the provisions of the Constitution relating to the militia. The correspondences which will be laid before you contain the requisite information on the subject. It is obvious that if the authority of the United States to call into service and command the militia for the public defense can be thus frustrated, even in a state of declared war and of course under apprehensions of invasion preceding war, they are not one nation for the purpose most of all requiring it, and that the public safety may have no other resource than in those large and permanent military establishments which are forbidden by the principles of our free government, and against the necessity of which the militia were meant to be a constitutional bulwark.

On the coasts and on the ocean the war has been as successful as circumstances inseparable from its early stages could promise. Our public ships and private cruisers, by their activity, and, where there was occasion, by their intrepidity, have made the enemy sensible of the difference between a reciprocity of captures and the long confinement of them to their side. Our trade, with little exception, has safely reached our ports, having been much favored in it by the course pursued by a squadron of our frigates under the command of Commodore Rodgers, and in the instance in which skill and bravery were more particularly tried with those of the enemy the American flag had an auspicious triumph. The frigate Constitution, commanded by Captain Hull, after a close and short engagement completely disabled and captured a British frigate, gaining for that officer and all on board a praise which can not be too liberally bestowed, not merely for the victory actually achieved, but for that prompt and cool exertion of commanding talents which, giving to courage its highest character, and to the force applied its full effect, proved that more could have been done in a contest requiring more.

Anxious to abridge the evils from which a state of war can not be exempt, I lost no time after it was declared in conveying to the British Government the terms on which its progress might be arrested, without awaiting the delays of a formal and final pacification, and our charge d'affaires at London was at the same time authorized to agree to an armistice founded upon them. These terms required that the orders in council should be repealed as they affected the United States, without a revival of blockades violating acknowledged rules, and that there should be an immediate discharge of American sea men from British ships, and a stop to impressment from American ships, with an understanding that an exclusion of the sea men of each nation from the ships of the other should be stipulated, and that the armistice should be improved into a definitive and comprehensive adjustment of depending controversies.

Although a repeal of the orders susceptible of explanations meeting the views of this Government had taken place before this pacific advance was communicated to that of Great Britain, the advance was declined from an avowed repugnance to a suspension of the practice of impressments during the armistice, and without any intimation that the arrangement proposed with regard to sea men would be accepted. Whether the subsequent communications from this Government, affording an occasion for reconsidering the subject on the part of Great Britain, will be viewed in a more favorable light or received in a more accommodating spirit remains to be known. It would be unwise to relax our measures in any respect on a presumption of such a result.

The documents from the Department of State which relate to this subject will give a view also of the propositions for an armistice which have been received here, one of them from the authorities at Halifax and in Canada, the other from the British Government itself through Admiral Warren, and of the grounds on which neither of them could be accepted.

Our affairs with France retain the posture which they held at my last communications to you. Notwithstanding the authorized expectations of an early as well as favorable issue to the discussions on foot, these have been procrastinated to the latest date. The only intervening occurrence meriting attention is the promulgation of a French decree purporting to be a definitive repeal of the Berlin and Milan decrees. This proceeding, although made the ground of the repeal of the British orders in council, is rendered by the time and manner of it liable to many objections.

The final communications from our special minister to Denmark afford further proofs of the good effects of his mission, and of the amicable disposition of the Danish Government. From Russia we have the satisfaction to receive assurances of continued friendship, and that it will not be affected by the rupture between the United States and Great Britain. Sweden also professes sentiments favorable to the subsisting harmony.

With the Barbary Powers, excepting that of Algiers, our affairs remain on the ordinary footing. The consul-general residing with that Regency has suddenly and without cause been banished, together with all the American citizens found there. Whether this was the transitory effect of capricious despotism or the first act of predetermined hostility is not ascertained. Precautions were taken by the consul on the latter supposition.

The Indian tribes not under foreign instigations remain at peace, and receive the civilizing attentions which have proved so beneficial to them.

With a view to that vigorous prosecution of the war to which our national faculties are adequate, the attention of Congress will be particularly drawn to the insufficiency of existing provisions for filling up the military establishment. Such is the happy condition of our country, arising from the facility of subsistence and the high wages for every species of occupation, that notwithstanding the augmented inducements provided at the last session, a partial success only has attended the recruiting service. The deficiency has been necessarily supplied during the campaign by other than regular troops, with all the inconveniences and expense incident to them. The remedy lies in establishing more favorably for the private soldier the proportion between his recompense and the term of his enlistment, and it is a subject which can not too soon or too seriously be taken into consideration.

The same insufficiency has been experienced in the provisions for volunteers made by an act of the last session. The recompense for the service required in this case is still less attractive than in the other, and although patriotism alone has sent into the field some valuable corps of that description, those alone who can afford the sacrifice can be reasonably expected to yield to that impulse.

It will merit consideration also whether as auxiliary to the security of our frontiers corps may not be advantageously organized with a restriction of their services to particular districts convenient to them, and whether the local and occasional services of mariners and others in the sea port towns under a similar organization would not be a provident addition to the means of their defense.

I recommend a provision for an increase of the general officers of the Army, the deficiency of which has been illustrated by the number and distance of separate commands which the course of the war and the advantage of the service have required.

And I can not press too strongly on the earliest attention of the Legislature the importance of the reorganization of the staff establishment with a view to render more distinct and definite the relations and responsibilities of its several departments. That there is room for improvements which will materially promote both economy and success in what appertains to the Army and the war is equally inculcated by the examples of other countries and by the experience of our own.

A revision of the militia laws for the purpose of rendering them more systematic and better adapting them to emergencies of the war is at this time particularly desirable.

Of the additional ships authorized to be fitted for service, two will be shortly ready to sail, a third is under repair, and delay will be avoided in the repair of the residue. Of the appropriations for the purchase of materials for ship building, the greater part has been applied to that object and the purchase will be continued with the balance.

The enterprising spirit which has characterized our naval force and its success, both in restraining insults and depredations on our coasts and in reprisals on the enemy, will not fail to recommend an enlargement of it.

There being reason to believe that the act prohibiting the acceptance of British licenses is not a sufficient guard against the use of them, for purposes favorable to the interests and views of the enemy, further provisions on that subject are highly important. Nor is it less so that penal enactments should be provided for cases of corrupt and perfidious intercourse with the enemy, not amounting to treason nor yet embraced by any statutory provisions.

A considerable number of American vessels which were in England when the revocation of the orders in council took place were laden with British manufactures under an erroneous impression that the non-importation act would immediately cease to operate, and have arrived in the United States. It did not appear proper to exercise on unforeseen cases of such magnitude the powers vested in the Treasury Department to mitigate forfeitures without previously affording to Congress an opportunity of making on the subject such provision as they may think proper. In their decision they will doubtless equally consult what is due to equitable considerations and to the public interest.

The receipts into the Treasury during the year ending on the 30th of September last have exceeded $16.5 millions, which have been sufficient to defray all the demands on the Treasury to that day, including a necessary reimbursement of near $3 millions of the principal of the public debt. In these receipts is included a sum of near $5.85 millions, received on account of the loans authorized by the acts of the last session; the whole sum actually obtained on loan amounts to $11 millions, the residue of which, being receivable subsequent to the 30th of September last, will, together with the current revenue, enable us to defray all the expenses of this year.

The duties on the late unexpected importations of British manufactures will render the revenue of the ensuing year more productive than could have been anticipated.

The situation of our country, fellow citizens, is not without its difficulties, though it abounds in animating considerations, of which the view here presented of our pecuniary resources is an example. With more than one nation we have serious and unsettled controversies, and with one, powerful in the means and habits of war, we are at war. The spirit and strength of the nation are nevertheless equal to the support of all its rights, and to carry it through all its trials. They can be met in that confidence.

Above all, we have the inestimable consolation of knowing that the war in which we are actually engaged is a war neither of ambition nor of vain glory; that it is waged not in violation of the rights of others, but in the maintenance of our own; that it was preceded by a patience without example under wrongs accumulating without end, and that it was finally not declared until every hope of averting it was extinguished by the transfer of the British scepter into new hands clinging to former councils, and until declarations were reiterated to the last hour, through the British envoy here, that the hostile edicts against our commercial rights and our maritime independence would not be revoked; nay, that they could not be revoked without violating the obligations of Great Britain to other powers, as well as to her own interests.

To have shrunk under such circumstances from manly resistance would have been a degradation blasting our best and proudest hopes; it would have struck us from the high rank where the virtuous struggles of our fathers had placed us, and have betrayed the magnificent legacy which we hold in trust for future generations. It would have acknowledged that on the element which forms three-fourths of the globe we inhabit, and where all independent nations have equal and common rights, the American people were not an independent people, but colonists and vassals.

It was at this moment and with such an alternative that war was chosen. The nation felt the necessity of it, and called for it. The appeal was accordingly made, in a just cause, to the Just and All-powerful Being who holds in His hand the chain of events and the destiny of nations.

It remains only that, faithful to ourselves, entangled in no connections with the views of other powers, and ever ready to accept peace from the hand of justice, we prosecute the war with united counsels and with the ample faculties of the nation until peace be so obtained and as the only means under the Divine blessing of speedily obtaining it.

***

State of the Union Address
James Madison
December 7, 1813
Fellow-Citizens of the Senate and House of Representatives:

In meeting you at the present interesting conjuncture it would have been highly satisfactory if I could have communicated a favorable result to the mission charged with negotiations for restoring peace. It was a just expectation, from the respect due to the distinguished Sovereign who had invited them by his offer of mediation, from the readiness with which the invitation was accepted on the part of the United States, and from the pledge to be found in an act of their Legislature for the liberality which their plenipotentiaries would carry into the negotiations, that no time would be lost by the British Government in embracing the experiment for hastening a stop to the effusion of blood. A prompt and cordial acceptance of the mediation on that side was the less to be doubted, as it was of a nature not to submit rights or pretensions on either side to the decision of an umpire, but to afford merely an opportunity, honorable and desirable to both, for discussing and, if possible, adjusting them for the interest of both.

The British cabinet, either mistaking our desire of peace for a dread of British power or misled by other fallacious calculations, has disappointed this reasonable anticipation. No communications from our envoys having reached us, no information on the subject has been received from that source; but it is known that the mediation was declined in the first instance, and there is no evidence, notwithstanding the lapse of time, that a change of disposition in the British councils has taken place or is to be expected.

Under such circumstances a nation proud of its rights and conscious of its strength has no choice but an exertion of the one in support of the other.

To this determination the best encouragement is derived from the success with which it has pleased the Almighty to bless our arms both on the land and on the water.

Whilst proofs have been continued of the enterprise and skill of our cruisers, public and private, on the ocean, and a trophy gained in the capture of a British by an American vessel of war, after an action giving celebrity to the name of the victorious commander, the great inland waters on which the enemy were also to be encountered have presented achievements of our naval arms as brilliant in their character as they have been important in their consequences.

On Lake Erie, the squadron under command of Captain Perry having met the British squadron of superior force, a sanguinary conflict ended in the capture of the whole. The conduct of that officer, adroit as it was daring, and which was so well seconded by his comrades, justly entitles them to the admiration and gratitude of their country, and will fill an early page in its naval annals with a victory never surpassed in luster, however much it may have been in magnitude.

On Lake Ontario the caution of the British commander, favored by contingencies, frustrated the efforts of the American commander to bring on a decisive action. Captain Chauncey was able, however, to establish an ascendancy on that important theater, and to prove by the manner in which he effected everything possible that opportunities only were wanted for a more shining display of his own talents and the gallantry of those under his command.

The success on Lake Erie having opened a passage to the territory of the enemy, the officer commanding the Northwestern army transferred the war thither, and rapidly pursuing the hostile troops, fleeing with their savage associates, forced a general action, which quickly terminated in the capture of the British and dispersion of the savage force.

This result is signally honorable to Major-General Harrison, by whose military talents it was prepared; to Colonel Johnson and his mounted volunteers, whose impetuous onset gave a decisive blow to the ranks of the enemy, and to the spirit of the volunteer militia, equally brave and patriotic, who bore an interesting part in the scene; more especially to the chief magistrate of Kentucky, at the head of them, whose heroism signalized in the war which established the independence of his country, sought at an advanced age a share in hardships and battles for maintaining its rights and its safely.

The effect of these successes has been to rescue the inhabitants of Michigan from their oppressions, aggravated by gross infractions of the capitulation which subjected them to a foreign power; to alienate the savages of numerous tribes from the enemy, by whom they were disappointed and abandoned, and to relieve an extensive region of country from a merciless warfare which desolated its frontiers and imposed on its citizens the most harassing services.

In consequences of our naval superiority on Lake Ontario and the opportunity afforded by it for concentrating our forces by water, operations which had been provisionally planned were set on foot against the possessions of the enemy on the St. Lawrence. Such, however, was the delay produced in the first instance by adverse weather of unusual violence and continuance and such the circumstances attending the final movements of the army, that the prospect, at one time so favorable, was not realized.

The cruelty of the enemy in enlisting the savages into a war with a nation desirous of mutual emulation in mitigating its calamities has not been confined to any one quarter. Wherever they could be turned against us no exertions to effect it have been spared. On our southwestern border the Creek tribes, who, yielding to our persevering endeavors, were gradually acquiring more civilized habits, became the unfortunate victims of seduction. A war in that quarter has been the consequence, infuriated by a bloody fanaticism recently propagated among them. It was necessary to crush such a war before it could spread among the contiguous tribes and before it could favor enterprises of the enemy into that vicinity. With this view a force was called into the service of the United States from the States of Georgia and Tennessee, which, with the nearest regular troops and other corps from the Massachussets Territory, might not only chastise the savages into present peace but make a lasting impression on their fears.

The progress of the expedition, as far as is yet known, corresponds with the martial zeal with which it was espoused, and the best hopes of a satisfactory issue are authorized by the complete success with which a well-planned enterprise was executed against a body of hostile savages by a detachment of the volunteer militia of Tennessee, under the gallant command of General Coffee, and by a still more important victory over a larger body of them, gained under the immediate command of Major-General Jackson, an officer equally distinguished for his patriotism and his military talents.

The systematic perseverance of the enemy in courting the aid of the savages in all quarters had the natural effect of kindling their ordinary propensity to war into a passion, which, even among those best disposed toward the United States, was ready, if not employed on our side, to be turned against us. A departure from our protracted forbearance to accept the services tendered by them has thus been forced upon us. But in yielding to it the retaliation has been mitigated as much as possible, both in its extent and in its character, stopping far short of the example of the enemy, who owe the advantages they have occasionally gained in battle chiefly to the number of their savage associates, and who have not controlled them either from their usual practice of indiscriminate massacre on defenseless inhabitants or from scenes of carnage without a parallel on prisoners to the British arms, guarded by all the laws of humanity and of honorable war. For these enormities the enemy are equally responsible, whether with the power to prevent them they want the will or with the knowledge of a want of power they still avail themselves of such instruments.

In other respects the enemy are pursuing a course which threatens consequences most afflicting to humanity.

A standing law of Great Britain naturalizes, as is well known, all aliens complying with conditions limited to a shorter period than those required by the United States, and naturalized subjects are in war employed by her Government in common with native subjects. In a contiguous British Province regulations promulgated since the commencement of the war compel citizens of the United States being there under certain circumstances to bear arms, whilst of the native emigrants from the United States, who compose much of the population of the Province, a number have actually borne arms against the United States within their limits, some of whom, after having done so, have become prisoners of war, and are now in our possession. The British commander in that Province, nevertheless, with the sanction, as appears, of his Government, thought proper to select from American prisoners of war and send to Great Britain for trial as criminals a number of individuals who had emigrated from the British dominions long prior to the state of war between the two nations, who had incorporated themselves into our political society in the modes recognized by the law and the practice of Great Britain, and who were made prisoners of war under the banners of their adopted country, fighting for its rights and its safety.

The protection due to these citizens requiring an effectual interposition in their behalf, a like number of British prisoners of war were put into confinement, with a notification that they would experience whatever violence might be committed on the American prisoners of war sent to Great Britain.

It was hoped that this necessary consequence of the step unadvisedly taken on the part of Great Britain would have led her Government to reflect on the inconsistencies of its conduct, and that a sympathy with the British, if not with the American, sufferers would have arrested the cruel career opened by its example.

This was unhappily not the case. In violation both of consistency and of humanity, American officers and non-commissioned officers in double the number of the British soldiers confined here were ordered into close confinement, with formal notice that in the event of a retaliation for the death which might be inflicted on the prisoners of war sent to Great Britain for trial the officers so confined would be put to death also. It was notified at the same time that the commanders of the British fleets and armies on our coasts are instructed in the same event to proceed with a destructive severity against our towns and their inhabitants.

That no doubt might be left with the enemy of our adherence to the retaliatory resort imposed on us, a correspondent number of British officers, prisoners of war in our hands, were immediately put into close confinement to abide the fate of those confined by the enemy, and the British Government was apprised of the determination of this Government to retaliate any other proceedings against us contrary to the legitimate modes of warfare.

It is fortunate for the United States that they have it in their power to meet the enemy in this deplorable contest as it is honorable to them that they do not join in it but under the most imperious obligations, and with the humane purpose of effectuating a return to the established usages of war.

The views of the French Government on the subjects which have been so long committed to negotiation have received no elucidation since the close of your late session. The minister plenipotentiary of the United States at Paris had not been enabled by proper opportunities to press the objects of his mission as prescribed by his instructions.

The militia being always to be regarded as the great bulwark of defense and security for free states, and the Constitution having wisely committed to the national authority a use of that force as the best provision against an unsafe military establishment, as well as a resource peculiarly adapted to a country having the extent and the exposure of the United States, I recommend to Congress a revision of the militia laws for the purpose of securing more effectually the services of all detachments called into the employment and placed under the Government of the United States.

It will deserve the consideration of Congress also whether among other improvements in the militia laws justice does not require a regulation, under due precautions, for defraying the expense incident to the first assembling as well as the subsequent movements of detachments called into the national service.

To give to our vessels of war, public and private, the requisite advantage in their cruises, it is of much importance that they should have, both for themselves and their prizes, the use of the ports and markets of friendly powers. With this view, I recommend to Congress the expediency of such legal provisions as may supply the defects or remove the doubts of the Executive authority, to allow to the cruisers of other powers at war with enemies of the United States such use of the American ports as may correspond with the privileges allowed by such powers to American cruisers.

During the year ending on the 30th of September last the receipts into the Treasury have exceeded $37.5 millions, of which near $24 millions were the produce of loans. After meeting all demands for the public service there remained in the Treasury on that day near $7 millions. Under the authority contained in the act of the 2nd of August last for borrowing $7.5 millions, that sum has been obtained on terms more favorable to the United States than those of the preceding loans made during the present year.

Further sums to a considerable amount will be necessary to be obtained in the same way during the ensuing year, and from the increased capital of the country, from the fidelity with which the public engagements have been kept and the public credit maintained, it may be expected on good grounds that the necessary pecuniary supplies will not be wanting.

The expenses of the current year, from the multiplied operations falling within it, have necessarily been extensive; but on a just estimate of the campaign in which the mass of them has been incurred the cost will not be found disproportionate to the advantages which have been gained. The campaign has, indeed, in its latter stages in one quarter been less favorable than was expected, but in addition to the importance of our naval success the progress of the campaign has been filled with incidents highly honorable to the American arms.

The attacks of the enemy on Craney Island, on Fort Meigs, on Sacketts Harbor, and on Sandusky have been vigorously and successfully repulsed; nor have they in any case succeeded on either frontier excepting when directed against the peaceable dwellings of individuals or villages unprepared or undefended.

On the other hand, the movements of the American Army have been followed by the reduction of York, and of Forts George, Erie, and Malden; by the recovery of Detroit and the extinction of the Indian war in the West, and by the occupancy or command of a large portion of Upper Canada. Battles have also been fought on the borders of the St. Lawrence, which, though not accomplishing their entire objects, reflect honor on the discipline and prowess of our soldiery, the best auguries of eventual victory. In the same scale are to be placed the late successes in the South over one of the most powerful, which had become one of the most hostile also, of the Indian tribes.

It would be improper to close this communication without expressing a thankfulness in which all ought to unite for the abundance; for the preservation of our internal tranquillity, and the stability of our free institutions, and, above all, for the light of divine truth and the protection of every man's conscience in the enjoyment of it. And although among our blessings we can not number an exemption from the evils of war, yet these will never be regarded as the greatest of evils by the friends of liberty and of the rights of nations. Our country has before preferred them to the degraded condition which was the alternative when the sword was drawn in the cause which gave birth to our national independence, and none who contemplate the magnitude and feel the value of that glorious event will shrink from a struggle to maintain the high and happy ground on which it placed the American people.

With all good citizens the justice and necessity of resisting wrongs and usurpations no longer to be borne will sufficiently outweigh the privations and sacrifices inseparable from a state of war. But it is a reflection, moreover, peculiarly consoling, that, whilst wars are generally aggravated by their baneful effects on the internal improvements and permanent prosperity of the nations engaged in them, such is the favored situation of the United States that the calamities of the contest into which they have been compelled to enter are mitigated by improvements and advantages of which the contest itself is the source.

If the war has increased the interruptions of our commerce, it has at the same time cherished and multiplied our manufactures so as to make us independent of all other countries for the more essential branches for which we ought to be dependent on none, and is even rapidly giving them an extent which will create additional staples in our future intercourse with foreign markets.

If much treasure has been expended, no inconsiderable portion of it has been applied to objects durable in their value and necessary to our permanent safety.

If the war has exposed us to increased spoliations on the ocean and to predatory incursions on the land, it has developed the national means of retaliating the former and of providing protection against the latter, demonstrating to all that every blow aimed at our maritime independence is an impulse accelerating the growth of our maritime power.

By diffusing through the mass of the nation the elements of military discipline and instruction; by augmenting and distributing warlike preparations applicable to future use; by evincing the zeal and valor with which they will be employed and the cheerfulness with which every necessary burden will be borne, a greater respect for our rights and a longer duration of our future peace are promised than could be expected without these proofs of the national character and resources.

The war has proved moreover that our free Government, like other free governments, though slow in its early movements, acquires in its progress a force proportioned to its freedom, and that the union of these States, the guardian of the freedom and safety of all and of each, is strengthened by every occasion that puts it to the test.

In fine, the war, with all its vicissitudes, is illustrating the capacity and the destiny of the United States to be a great, a flourishing, and a powerful nation, worthy of the friendship which it is disposed to cultivate with all others, and authorized by its own example to require from all an observance of the laws of justice and reciprocity. Beyond these their claims have never extended, and in contending for these we behold a subject for our congratulations in the daily testimonies of increasing harmony throughout the nation, and may humbly repose our trust in the smiles of Heaven on so righteous a cause.

***

State of the Union Address
James Madison
September 20, 1814
Fellow-Citizens of the Senate and House of Representatives:

Notwithstanding the early day which had been fixed for your session of the present year, I was induced to call you together still sooner, as well that any inadequacy in the existing provisions for the wants of the Treasury might be supplied as that no delay might happen in providing for the result of the negotiations on foot with Great Britain, whether it should require arrangements adapted to a return of peace or further and more effective provisions for prosecuting the war.

That result is not yet known. If, on the one hand, the repeal of the orders in council and the general pacification in Europe, which withdrew the occasion on which impressments from American vessels were practiced, suggest expectations that peace and amity may be reestablished, we are compelled, on the other hand, by the refusal of the British Government to accept the offered mediation of the Emperor of Russia, by the delays in giving effect to its own proposal of a direct negotiation, and, above all, by the principles and manner in which the war is now avowedly carried on to infer that a spirit of hostility is indulged more violent than ever against the rights and prosperity of this country.

This increased violence is best explained by the two important circumstances that the great contest in Europe for an equilibrium guaranteeing all its States against the ambition of any has been closed without any check on the over-bearing power of Great Britain on the ocean, and it has left in her hands disposable armaments, with which, forgetting the difficulties of a remote war with a free people, and yielding to the intoxication of success, with the example of a great victim to it before her eyes, she cherishes hopes of still further aggrandizing a power already formidable in its abuses to the tranquillity of the civilized and commercial world.

But whatever may have inspired the enemy with these more violent purposes, the public councils of a nation more able to maintain than it was to require its independence, and with a devotion to it rendered more ardently by the experience of its blessings, can never deliberate but on the means most effectual for defeating the extravagant views or unwarrantable passions with which alone the war can now be pursued against us.

In the events of the present campaign the enemy, with all his augmented means and wanton use of them, has little ground for exultation, unless he can feel it in the success of his recent enterprises against this metropolis and the neighboring town of Alexandria, from both of which his retreats were as precipitate as his attempts were bold and fortunate. In his other incursions on our Atlantic frontier his progress, often checked and chastised by the martial spirit of the neighboring citizens, has had more effect in distressing individuals and in dishonoring his arms than in promoting any object of legitimate warfare; and in the two instances mentioned, however deeply to be regretted on our part, he will find in his transient success, which interrupted for a moment only the ordinary business at the seat of Government, no compensation for the loss of character with the world by his violations of private property and by his destruction of public edifices protected as monuments of the arts by the laws of civilized warfare.

On our side we can appeal to a series of achievements which have given new luster to the American arms. Besides the brilliant incidents in the minor operations of the campaign, the splendid victories gained on the Canadian side of the Niagara by the American forces under Major-General Brown and Brigadiers Scott and Gaines have gained for these heroes and their emulating companions the most unfading laurels, and, having triumphantly tested the progressive discipline of the American soldiery, have taught the enemy that the longer he protracts his hostile efforts the more certain and decisive will be his final discomfiture.

On our southern border victory has continued also to follow the American standard. The bold and skillful operations of Major-General Jackson, conducting troops drawn from the militia of the States least distant, particularly Tennessee, have subdued the principal tribes of hostile savages, and, by establishing a peace with them, preceded by recent and exemplary chastisement, has best guarded against the mischief of their cooperations with the British enterprises which may be planned against that quarter of our country. Important tribes of Indians on our northwestern frontier have also acceded to stipulations which bind them to the interests of the United States and to consider our enemy as theirs also.

In the recent attempt of the enemy on the city of Baltimore, defended by militia and volunteers, aided by a small body of regulars and sea men, he was received with a spirit which produced a rapid retreat to his ships, whilst concurrent attack by a large fleet was successfully resisted by the steady and well-directed fire of the fort and batteries opposed to it.

In another recent attack by a powerful force on our troops at Plattsburg, of which regulars made a part only, the enemy, after a perseverance for many hours, was finally compelled to seek safety in a hasty retreat, with our gallant bands pressing upon them.

On the Lakes, so much contested throughout the war, the great exertions for the command made on our part have been well repaid. On Lake Ontario our squadron is now and has been for some time in a condition to confine that of the enemy to his own port, and to favor the operations of our land forces on that frontier.

A part of the squadron on Lake Erie has been extended into Lake Huron, and has produced the advantage of displaying our command on that lake also. One object of the expedition was the reduction of Mackinaw, which followed with the loss of a few brave men, among whom was an officer justly distinguished for his gallant exploits. The expedition, ably conducted by both the land and the naval commanders, was otherwise highly valuable in its effects.

On Lake Champlain, where our superiority had for some time been undisputed, the British squadron lately came into action with the American, commanded by Captain Macdonough. It issued in the capture of the whole of the enemy's ships. The best praise for this officer and his intrepid comrades is in the likeness of his triumph to the illustrious victory which immortalized another officer and established at a critical moment our command of another lake.

On the ocean the pride of our naval arms had been amply supported. A second frigate has indeed fallen into the hands of the enemy, but the loss is hidden in the blaze of heroism with which she was defended. Captain Porter, who commanded her, and whose previous career had been distinguished by daring enterprise and by fertility of genius, maintained a sanguinary contest against two ships, one of them superior to his own, and under other severe disadvantages, 'til humanity tore down the colors which valor had nailed to the mast. This officer and his brave comrades have added much to the rising glory of the American flag, and have merited all the effusions of gratitude which their country is ever ready to bestow on the champions of its rights and of its safety.

Two smaller vessels of war have also become prizes to the enemy, but by a superiority of force which sufficiently vindicates the reputation of their commanders, whilst two others, one commanded by Captain Warrington, the other by Captain Blakely, have captured British ships of the same class with a gallantry and good conduct which entitle them and their companions to a just share in the praise of their country.

In spite of the naval force of the enemy accumulated on our coasts, our private cruisers also have not ceased to annoy his commerce and to bring their rich prizes into our ports, contributing thus, with other proofs, to demonstrate the incompetency and illegality of a blockade the proclamation of which is made the pretext for vexing and discouraging the commerce of neutral powers with the United States.

To meet the extended and diversified warfare adopted by the enemy, great bodies of militia have been taken into service for the public defense, and great expenses incurred. That the defense everywhere may be both more convenient and more economical, Congress will see the necessity of immediate measures for filling the ranks of the Regular Army and of enlarging the provision for special corps, mounted and unmounted, to be engaged for longer periods of service than are due from the militia. I earnestly renew, at the same time, a recommendation of such changes in the system of the militia as, by classing and disciplining for the most prompt and active service the portions most capable of it, will give to that great resource for the public safety all the requisite energy and efficiency.

The moneys received into the Treasury during the nine months ending on the 30th day of June last amounted to $32 millions, of which near $11 millions were the proceeds of the public revenue and the remainder derived from loans. The disbursements for public expenditures during the same period exceeded $34 millions, and left in the Treasury on the first day of July near $5 millions. The demands during the remainder of the present year already authorized by Congress and the expenses incident to an extension of the operations of the war will render it necessary that large sums should be provided to meet them.

From this view of the national affairs Congress will be urged to take up without delay as well the subject of pecuniary supplies as that of military force, and on a scale commensurate with the extent and the character which the war has assumed. It is not to be disguised that the situation of our country calls for its greatest efforts.

Our enemy is powerful in men and in money, on the land and on the water. Availing himself of fortuitous advantages, he is aiming with his undivided force a deadly blow at our growing prosperity, perhaps at our national existence. He has avowed his purpose of trampling on the usages of civilized warfare, and given earnests of it in the plunder and wanton destruction of private property. In his pride of maritime dominion and in his thirst of commercial monopoly he strikes with peculiar animosity at the progress of our navigation and of our manufactures. His barbarous policy has not even spared those monuments of the arts and models of taste with which our country had enriched and embellished its infant metropolis. From such an adversary hostility in its greatest force and in its worst forms may be looked for.

The American people will face it with the undaunted spirit which in their revolutionary struggle defeated his unrighteous projects. His threats and his barbarities, instead of dismay, will kindle in every bosom an indignation not to be extinguished but in the disaster and expulsion of such cruel invaders.

In providing the means necessary the National Legislature will not distrust the heroic and enlightened patriotism of its constituents. They will cheerfully and proudly bear every burden of every kind which the safety and honor of the nation demand. We have seen them everywhere paying their taxes, direct and indirect, with the greatest promptness and alacrity. We see them rushing with enthusiasm to the scenes where danger and duty call. In offering their blood they give the surest pledge that no other tribute will be withheld.

Having forborne to declare war until to other aggressions had been added the capture of near one thousand American vessels and the impressment of thousands of American sea faring citizens, and until a final declaration had been made by the Government of Great Britain that her hostile orders against our commerce would not be revoked but on conditions as impossible as unjust, whilst it was known that these orders would not otherwise cease but with a war which had lasted nearly twenty years, and which, according to appearances at that time, might last as many more; having manifested on every occasion and in every proper mode a sincere desire to arrest the effusion of blood and meet our enemy on the ground of justice and reconciliation, our beloved country, in still opposing to his persevering hostility all its energies, with an undiminished disposition toward peace and friendship on honorable terms, must carry with it the good wishes of the impartial world and the best hopes of support from an omnipotent and kind Providence.

***

State of the Union Address
James Madison
December 5, 1815
Fellow-Citizens of the Senate and House of Representatives:

I have the satisfaction on our present meeting of being able to communicate the successful termination of the war which had been commenced against the United States by the Regency of Algiers. The squadron in advance on that service, under Commodore Decatur, lost not a moment after its arrival in the Mediterranean in seeking the naval force of the enemy then cruising in that sea, and succeeded in capturing two of his ships, one of them the principal ship, commanded by the Algerine admiral. The high character of the American commander was brilliantly sustained on the occasion which brought his own ship into close action with that of his adversary, as was the accustomed gallantry of all the officers and men actually engaged. Having prepared the way by this demonstration of American skill and prowess, he hastened to the port of Algiers, where peace was promptly yielded to his victorious force.

In the terms stipulated the rights and honor of the United States were particularly consulted by a perpetual relinquishment on the part of the Dey of all pretensions to tribute from them. The impressions which have thus been made, strengthened as they will have been by subsequent transactions with the Regencies of Tunis and of Tripoli by the appearance of the larger force which followed under Commodore Bainbridge, the chief in command of the expedition, and by the judicious precautionary arrangements left by him in that quarter, afford a reasonable prospect of future security for the valuable portion of our commerce which passes within reach of the Barbary cruisers.

It is another source of satisfaction that the treaty of peace with Great Britain has been succeeded by a convention on the subject of commerce concluded by the plenipotentiaries of the two countries. In this result a disposition is manifested on the part of that nation corresponding with the disposition of the United States, which it may be hoped will be improved into liberal arrangements on other subjects on which the parties have mutual interests, or which might endanger their future harmony. Congress will decide on the expediency of promoting such a sequel by giving effect to the measure of confining the American navigation to American sea men--a measure which, at the same time that it might have that conciliatory tendency, would have the further advantage of increasing the independence of our navigation and the resources for our maritime defense.

In conformity with the articles in the treaty of Ghent relating to the Indians, as well as with a view to the tranquillity of our western and northwestern frontiers, measures were taken to establish an immediate peace with the several tribes who had been engaged in hostilities against the United States. Such of them as were invited to Detroit acceded readily to a renewal of the former treaties of friendship. Of the other tribes who were invited to a station on the Mississippi the greater number have also accepted the peace offered to them. The residue, consisting of the more distant tribes or parts of tribes, remain to be brought over by further explanations, or by such other means as may be adapted to the dispositions they may finally disclose.

The Indian tribes within and bordering on the southern frontier, whom a cruel war on their part had compelled us to chastise into peace, have latterly shown a restlessness which has called for preparatory measures for repressing it, and for protecting the commissioners engaged in carrying the terms of the peace into execution.

The execution of the act for fixing the military peace establishment has been attended with difficulties which even now can only be overcome by legislative aid. The selection of officers, the payment and discharge of the troops enlisted for the war, the payment of the retained troops and their reunion from detached and distant stations, the collection and security of the public property in the Quartermaster, Commissary, and Ordnance departments, and the constant medical assistance required in hospitals and garrisons rendered a complete execution of the act impracticable on the 1st of May, the period more immediately contemplated. As soon, however, as circumstances would permit, and as far as it has been practicable consistently with the public interests, the reduction of the Army has been accomplished; but the appropriations for its pay and for other branches of the military service having proved inadequate, the earliest attention to that subject will be necessary; and the expediency of continuing upon the peace establishment the staff officers who have hitherto been provisionally retained is also recommended to the consideration of Congress.

In the performance of the Executive duty upon this occasion there has not been wanting a just sensibility to the merits of the American Army during the late war; but the obvious policy and design in fixing an efficient military peace establishment did not afford an opportunity to distinguish the aged and infirm on account of their past services nor the wounded and disabled on account of their present sufferings.

The extent of the reduction, indeed, unavoidably involved the exclusion of many meritorious officers of every rank from the service of their country; and so equal as well as so numerous were the claims to attention that a decision by the standard of comparative merit could seldom be attained. Judged, however, in candor by a general standard of positive merit, the Army Register will, it is believed, do honor to the establishment, while the case of those officers whose names are not included in it devolves with the strongest interest upon the legislative authority for such provisions as shall be deemed the best calculated to give support and solace to the veteran and the invalid, to display the beneficence as well as the justice of the Government, and to inspire a martial zeal for the public service upon every future emergency.

Although the embarrassments arising from the want of an uniform national currency have not been diminished since the adjournment of Congress, great satisfaction has been derived in contemplating the revival of the public credit and the efficiency of the public resources. The receipts into the Treasury from the various branches of revenue during the nine months ending on the 30th of September last have been estimated at $12.5 millions; the issues of Treasury notes of every denomination during the same period amounted to the sum of $14 millions, and there was also obtained upon loan during the same period a sum of $9 millions, of which the sum of $6 millions was subscribed in cash and the sum of $3 millions in Treasury notes.

With these means, added to the sum of $1.5 millions, being the balance of money in the Treasury on the 1st day of January, there has been paid between the 1st of January and the 1st of October on account of the appropriations of the preceding and of the present year (exclusively of the amount of the Treasury notes subscribed to the loan and of the amount redeemed in the payment of duties and taxes) the aggregate sum of $33.5 millions, leaving a balance then in the Treasury estimated at the sum of $3 millions. Independent, however of the arrearages due for military services and supplies, it is presumed that a further sum of $5 millions, including the interest on the public debt payable on the 1st of January next, will be demanded at the Treasury to complete the expenditures of the present year, and for which the existing ways and means will sufficiently provide.

The national debt, as it was ascertained on the 1st of October last, amounted in the whole to the sum of $120 millions, consisting of the unredeemed balance of the debt contracted before the late war ($39 millions), the amount of the funded debt contracted in consequence of the war ($64 millions), and the amount of the unfunded and floating debt, including the various issues of Treasury notes, $17 millions, which is in gradual course of payment.

There will probably be some addition to the public debt upon the liquidation of various claims which are depending, and a conciliatory disposition on the part of Congress may lead honorably and advantageously to an equitable arrangement of the militia expenses incurred by the several States without the previous sanction or authority of the Government of the United States; but when it is considered that the new as well as the old portion of the debt has been contracted in the assertion of the national rights and independence, and when it is recollected that the public expenditures, not being exclusively bestowed upon subjects of a transient nature, will long be visible in the number and equipments of the American Navy, in the military works for the defense of our harbors and our frontiers, and in the supplies of our arsenals and magazines the amount will bear a gratifying comparison with the objects which have been attained, as well as with the resources of the country.

The arrangements of the finances with a view to the receipts and expenditures of a permanent peace establishment will necessarily enter into the deliberations of Congress during the present session. It is true that the improved condition of the public revenue will not only afford the means of maintaining the faith of the Government with its creditors inviolate, and of prosecuting successfully the measures of the most liberal policy, but will also justify an immediate alleviation of the burdens imposed by the necessities of the war.

It is, however, essential to every modification of the finances that the benefits of an uniform national currency should be restored to the community. The absence of the precious metals will, it is believed, be a temporary evil, but until they can again be rendered the general medium of exchange it devolves on the wisdom of Congress to provide a substitute which shall equally engage the confidence and accommodate the wants of the citizens throughout the Union. If the operation of the State banks can not produce this result, the probable operation of a national bank will merit consideration; and if neither of these expedients be deemed effectual it may become necessary to ascertain the terms upon which the notes of the Government (no longer required as an instrument of credit) shall be issued upon motives of general policy as a common medium of circulation.

Notwithstanding the security for future repose which the United States ought to find in their love of peace and their constant respect for the rights of other nations, the character of the times particularly inculcates the lesson that, whether to prevent or repel danger, we ought not to be unprepared for it. This consideration will sufficiently recommend to Congress a liberal provision for the immediate extension and gradual completion of the works of defense, both fixed and floating, on our maritime frontier, and an adequate provision for guarding our inland frontier against dangers to which certain portions of it may continue to be exposed.

As an improvement in our military establishment, it will deserve the consideration of Congress whether a corps of invalids might not be so organized and employed as at once to aid in the support of meritorious individuals excluded by age or infirmities from the existing establishment, and to procure to the public the benefit of their stationary services and of their exemplary discipline.

I recommend also an enlargement of the Military Academy already established, and the establishment of others in other sections of the Union; and I can not press too much on the attention of Congress such a classification and organization of the militia as will most effectually render it the safeguard of a free state. If experience has shewn in the recent splendid achievements of militia the value of this resource for the public defense, it has shewn also the importance of that skill in the use of arms and that familiarity with the essential rules of discipline which can not be expected from the regulations now in force.

With this subject is intimately connected the necessity of accommodating the laws in every respect to the great object of enabling the political authority of the Union to employ promptly and effectually the physical power of the Union in the cases designated by the Constitution.

The signal services which have been rendered by our Navy and the capacities it has developed for successful cooperation in the national defense will give to that portion of the public force its full value in the eyes of Congress, at an epoch which calls for the constant vigilance of all governments. To preserve the ships now in a sound state, to complete those already contemplated, to provide amply the imperishable materials for prompt augmentations, and to improve the existing arrangements into more advantageous establishments for the construction, the repairs, and the security of vessels of war is dictated by the soundest policy.

In adjusting the duties on imports to the object of revenue the influence of the tariff on manufactures will necessarily present itself for consideration. However wise the theory may be which leaves to the sagacity and interest of individuals the application of their industry and resources, there are in this as in other cases exceptions to the general rule. Besides the condition which the theory itself implies of reciprocal adoption by other nations, experience teaches that so many circumstances must concur in introducing and maturing manufacturing establishments, especially of the more complicated kinds, that a country may remain long without them, although sufficiently advanced and in some respects even peculiarly fitted for carrying them on with success. Under circumstances giving a powerful impulse to manufacturing industry it has made among us a progress and exhibited an efficiency which justify the belief that with a protection not more than is due to the enterprising citizens whose interests are now at stake it will become at an early day not only safe against occasional competitions from abroad, but a source of domestic wealth and even of external commerce.

In selecting the branches more especially entitled to the public patronage a preference is obviously claimed by such as will relieve the United States from a dependence on foreign supplies, ever subject to casual failures, for articles necessary for the public defense or connected with the primary wants of individuals. It will be an additional recommendation of particular manufactures where the materials for them are extensively drawn from our agriculture, and consequently impart and insure to that great fund of national prosperity and independence an encouragement which can not fail to be rewarded.

Among the means of advancing the public interest the occasion is a proper one for recalling the attention of Congress to the great importance of establishing throughout our country the roads and canals which can best be executed under the national authority. No objects within the circle of political economy so richly repay the expense bestowed on them; there are none the utility of which is more universally ascertained and acknowledged; none that do more honor to the governments whose wise and enlarged patriotism duly appreciates them. Nor is there any country which presents a field where nature invites more the art of man to complete her own work for his accommodation and benefit.

These considerations are strengthened, moreover, by the political effect of these facilities for intercommunication in bringing and binding more closely together the various parts of our extended confederacy. Whilst the States individually, with a laudable enterprise and emulation, avail themselves of their local advantages by new roads, by navigable canals, and by improving the streams susceptible of navigation, the General Government is the more urged to similar undertakings, requiring a national jurisdiction and national means, by the prospect of thus systematically completing so inestimable a work; and it is a happy reflection that any defect of constitutional authority which may be encountered can be supplied in a mode which the Constitution itself has providently pointed out.

The present is a favorable season also for bringing again into view the establishment of a national seminary of learning within the District of Columbia, and with means drawn from the property therein, subject to the authority of the General Government. Such an institution claims the patronage of Congress as a monument of their solicitude for the advancement of knowledge, without which the blessings of liberty can not be fully enjoyed or long preserved; as a model instructive in the formation of other seminaries; as a nursery of enlightened preceptors, and as a central resort of youth and genius from every part of their country, diffusing on their return examples of those national feelings, those liberal sentiments, and those congenial manners which contribute cement to our Union and strength to the great political fabric of which that is the foundation.

In closing this communication I ought not to repress a sensibility, in which you will unite, to the happy lot of our country and to the goodness of a superintending Providence, to which we are indebted for it. Whilst other portions of mankind are laboring under the distresses of war or struggling with adversity in other forms, the United States are in the tranquil enjoyment of prosperous and honorable peace. In reviewing the scenes through which it has been attained we can rejoice in the proofs given that our political institutions, founded in human rights and framed for their preservation, are equal to the severest trials of war, as well adapted to the ordinary periods of repose.

As fruits of this experience and of the reputation acquired by the American arms on the land and on the water, the nation finds itself possessed of a growing respect abroad and of a just confidence in itself, which are among the best pledges for its peaceful career. Under other aspects of our country the strongest features of its flourishing condition are seen in a population rapidly increasing on a territory as productive as it is extensive; in a general industry and fertile ingenuity which find their ample rewards, and in an affluent revenue which admits a reduction of the public burdens without withdrawing the means of sustaining the public credit, of gradually discharging the public debt, of providing for the necessary defensive and precautionary establishments, and of patronizing in every authorized mode undertakings conducive to the aggregate wealth and individual comfort of our citizens.

It remains for the guardians of the public welfare to persevere in that justice and good will toward other nations which invite a return of these sentiments toward the United States; to cherish institutions which guarantee their safety and their liberties, civil and religious; and to combine with a liberal system of foreign commerce an improvement of the national advantages and a protection and extension of the independent resources of our highly favored and happy country.

In all measures having such objects my faithful cooperation will be afforded.

***

State of the Union Address
James Madison
December 3, 1816
Fellow-Citizens of the Senate and House of Representatives:

In reviewing the present state of our country, our attention cannot be withheld from the effect produced by peculiar seasons which have very generally impaired the annual gifts of the earth and threatened scarcity in particular districts. Such, however, is the variety of soils, of climates, and of products within our extensive limits that the aggregate resources for subsistence are more than sufficient for the aggregate wants. And as far as an economy of consumption, more than usual, may be necessary, our thankfulness is due to Providence for what is far more than a compensation, in the remarkable health which has distinguished the present year.

Amidst the advantages which have succeeded the peace of Europe, and that of the United States with Great Britain, in a general invigoration of industry among us and in the extension of our commerce, the value of which is more and more disclosing itself to commercial nations, it is to be regretted that a depression is experienced by particular branches of our manufactures and by a portion of our navigation. As the first proceeds in an essential degree from an excess of imported merchandise, which carries a check in its own tendency, the cause in its present extent can not be very long in duration. The evil will not, however, be viewed by Congress without a recollection that manufacturing establishments, if suffered to sink too low or languish too long, may not revive after the causes shall have ceased, and that in the vicissitudes of human affairs situations may recur in which a dependence on foreign sources for indispensable supplies may be among the most serious embarrassments.

The depressed state of our navigation is to be ascribed in a material degree to its exclusion from the colonial ports of the nation most extensively connected with us in commerce, and from the indirect operation of that exclusion.

Previous to the late convention at London between the United States and Great Britain the relative state of the navigation laws of the two countries, growing out of the treaty of 1794, had given to the British navigation a material advantage over the American in the intercourse between the American ports and British ports in Europe. The convention of London equalized the laws of the two countries relating to those ports, leaving the intercourse between our ports and the ports of the British colonies subject, as before, to the respective regulations of the parties. The British Government enforcing now regulations which prohibit a trade between its colonies and the United States in American vessels, whilst they permit a trade in British vessels, the American navigation loses accordingly, and the loss is augmented by the advantage which is given to the British competition over the American in the navigation between our ports and British ports in Europe by the circuitous voyages enjoyed by the one and not enjoyed by the other.

The reasonableness of the rule of reciprocity applied to one branch of the commercial intercourse has been pressed on our part as equally applicable to both branches; but it is ascertained that the British cabinet declines all negotiation on the subject, with a disavowal, however, of any disposition to view in an unfriendly light whatever countervailing regulations the United States may oppose to the regulations of which they complain. The wisdom of the Legislature will decide on the course which, under these circumstances, is prescribed by a joint regard to the amicable relations between the two nations and to the just interests of the United States.

I have the satisfaction to state, generally, that we remain in amity with foreign powers.

An occurrence has indeed taken place in the Gulf of Mexico which, if sanctioned by the Spanish Government, may make an exception as to that power. According to the report of our naval commander on that station, one of our public armed vessels was attacked by an over-powering force under a Spanish commander, and the American flag, with the officers and crew, insulted in a manner calling for prompt reparation. This has been demanded. In the mean time a frigate and a smaller vessel of war have been ordered into that Gulf for the protection of our commerce. It would be improper to omit that the representative of His Catholic Majesty in the United States lost no time in giving the strongest assurances that no hostile order could have emanated from his Government, and that it will be as ready to do as to expect whatever the nature of the case and the friendly relations of the two countries shall be found to require.

The posture of our affairs with Algiers at the present moment is not known. The Dey, drawing pretexts from circumstances for which the United States were not answerable, addressed a letter to this Government declaring the treaty last concluded with him to have been annulled by our violation of it, and presenting as the alternative war or a renewal of the former treaty, which stipulated, among other things, an annual tribute. The answer, with an explicit declaration that the United States preferred war to tribute, required his recognition and observance of the treaty last made, which abolishes tribute and the slavery of our captured citizens. The result of the answer has not been received. Should he renew his warfare on our commerce, we rely on the protection it will find in our naval force actually in the Mediterranean.

With the other Barbary States our affairs have undergone no change.

The Indian tribes within our limits appear also disposed to remain at peace. From several of them purchases of lands have been made particularly favorable to the wishes and security of our frontier settlements, as well as to the general interests of the nation. In some instances the titles, though not supported by due proof, and clashing those of one tribe with the claims of another, have been extinguished by double purchases, the benevolent policy of the United States preferring the augmented expense to the hazard of doing injustice or to the enforcement of justice against a feeble and untutored people by means involving or threatening an effusion of blood.

I am happy to add that the tranquillity which has been restored among the tribes themselves, as well as between them and our own population, will favor the resumption of the work of civilization which had made an encouraging progress among some tribes, and that the facility is increasing for extending that divided and individual ownership, which exists now in movable property only, to the soil itself, and of thus establishing in the culture and improvement of it the true foundation for a transit from the habits of the savage to the arts and comforts of social life.

As a subject of the highest importance to the national welfare, I must again earnestly recommend to the consideration of Congress a reorganization of the militia on a plan which will form it into classes according to the periods of life more or less adapted to military services. An efficient militia is authorized and contemplated by the

Constitution and required by the spirit and safety of free government. The present organization of our militia is universally regarded as less efficient than it ought to be made, and no organization can be better calculated to give to it its due force than a classification which will assign the foremost place in the defense of the country to that portion of its citizens whose activity and animation best enable them to rally to its standard. Besides the consideration that a time of peace is the time when the change can be made with most convenience and equity, it will now be aided by the experience of a recent war in which the militia bore so interesting a part.

Congress will call to mind that no adequate provision has yet been made for the uniformity of weights and measures also contemplated by the Constitution. The great utility of a standard fixed in its nature and founded on the easy rule of decimal proportions is sufficiently obvious. It led the Government at an early stage to preparatory steps for introducing it, and a completion of the work will be a just title to the public gratitude.

The importance which I have attached to the establishment of a university within this District on a scale and for objects worthy of the American nation induces me to renew my recommendation of it to the favorable consideration of Congress. And I particularly invite again their attention to the expediency of exercising their existing powers, and, where necessary, of resorting to the prescribed mode of enlarging them, in order to effectuate a comprehensive system of roads and canals, such as will have the effect of drawing more closely together every part of our country by promoting intercourse and improvements and by increasing the share of every part in the common stock of national prosperity.

Occurrences having taken place which shew that the statutory provisions for the dispensation of criminal justice are deficient in relation both to places and to persons under the exclusive cognizance of the national authority, an amendment of the law embracing such cases will merit the earliest attention of the Legislature. It will be a seasonable occasion also for inquiring how far legislative interposition may be further requisite in providing penalties for offenses designated in the Constitution or in the statutes, and to which either no penalties are annexed or none with sufficient certainty. And I submit to the wisdom of Congress whether a more enlarged revisal of the criminal code be not expedient for the purpose of mitigating in certain cases penalties which were adopted into it antecedent to experiment and examples which justify and recommend a more lenient policy.

The United States, having been the first to abolish within the extent of their authority the transportation of the natives of Africa into slavery, by prohibiting the introduction of slaves and by punishing their citizens participating in the traffic, can not but be gratified at the progress made by concurrent efforts of other nations toward a general suppression of so great an evil. They must feel at the same time the greater solicitude to give the fullest efficacy to their own regulations. With that view, the interposition of Congress appears to be required by the violations and evasions which it is suggested are chargeable on unworthy citizens who mingle in the slave trade under foreign flags and with foreign ports, and by collusive importations of slaves into the United States through adjoining ports and territories. I present the subject to Congress with a full assurance of their disposition to apply all the remedy which can be afforded by an amendment of the law. The regulations which were intended to guard against abuses of a kindred character in the trade between the several States ought also to be rendered more effectual for their humane object.

To these recommendations I add, for the consideration of Congress, the expediency of a remodification of the judiciary establishment, and of an additional department in the executive branch of the Government.

The first is called for by the accruing business which necessarily swells the duties of the Federal courts, and by the great and widening space within which justice is to be dispensed by them. The time seems to have arrived which claims for members of the Supreme Court a relief from itinerary fatigues, incompatible as well with the age which a portion of them will always have attained as with the researches and preparations which are due to their stations and to the juridical reputation of their country. And considerations equally cogent require a more convenient organization of the subordinate tribunals, which may be accomplished without an objectionable increase of the number or expense of the judges.

The extent and variety of executive business also accumulating with the progress of our country and its growing population call for an additional department, to be charged with duties now over-burdening other departments and with such as have not been annexed to any department.

The course of experience recommends, as another improvement in the executive establishment, that the provision for the station of Attorney-General, whose residence at the seat of Government, official connections with it, and the management of the public business before the judiciary preclude an extensive participation in professional emoluments, be made more adequate to his services and his relinquishments, and that, with a view to his reasonable accommodation and to a proper depository of his official opinions and proceedings, there be included in the provision the usual appurtenances to a public office.

In directing the legislative attention to the state of the finances it is a subject of great gratification to find that even within the short period which has elapsed since the return of peace the revenue has far exceeded all the current demands upon the Treasury, and that under any probable diminution of its future annual products which the vicissitudes of commerce may occasion it will afford an ample fund for the effectual and early extinguishment of the public debt. It has been estimated that during the year 1816 the actual receipts of revenue at the Treasury, including the balance at the commencement of the year, and excluding the proceeds of loans and Treasury notes, will amount to about the sum of $47 millions; that during the same year the actual payments at the Treasury, including the payment of the arrearages of the War Department as well as the payment of a considerable excess beyond the annual appropriations, will amount to about the sum of $38 millions, and that consequently at the close of the year there will be a surplus in the Treasury of about the sum of $9 millions.

The operations of the Treasury continued to be obstructed by difficulties arising from the condition of the national currency, but they have nevertheless been effectual to a beneficial extent in the reduction of the public debt and the establishment of the public credit. The floating debt of Treasury notes and temporary loans will soon be entirely discharged. The aggregate of the funded debt, composed of debts incurred during the wars of 1776 and 1812, has been estimated with reference to the first of January next at a sum not exceeding $110 millions. The ordinary annual expenses of the Government for the maintenance of all its institutions, civil, military, and naval, have been estimated at a sum greater than $20 millions, and the permanent revenue to be derived from all the existing sources has been estimated at a sum of $25 millions.

Upon this general view of the subject it is obvious that there is only wanting to the fiscal prosperity of the Government the restoration of an uniform medium of exchange. The resources and the faith of the nation, displayed in the system which Congress has established, insure respect and confidence both at home and abroad. The local accumulations of the revenue have already enabled the Treasury to meet the public engagements in the local currency of most of the States, and it is expected that the same cause will produce the same effect throughout the Union; but for the interests of the community at large, as well as for the purposes of the Treasury, it is essential that the nation should possess a currency of equal value, credit, and use wherever it may circulate. The Constitution has intrusted Congress exclusively with the power of creating and regulating a currency of that description, and the measures which were taken during the last session in execution of the power give every promise of success. The Bank of the United States has been organized under auspices the most favorable, and can not fail to be an important auxiliary to those measures.

For a more enlarged view of the public finances, with a view of the measures pursued by the Treasury Department previous to the resignation of the late Secretary, I transmit an extract from the last report of that officer. Congress will perceive in it ample proofs of the solid foundation on which the financial prosperity of the nation rests, and will do justice to the distinguished ability and successful exertions with which the duties of the Department were executed during a period remarkable for its difficulties and its peculiar perplexities.

The period of my retiring from the public service being at little distance, I shall find no occasion more proper than the present for expressing to my fellow citizens my deep sense of the continued confidence and kind support which I have received from them. My grateful recollection of these distinguished marks of their favorable regard can never cease, and with the consciousness that, if I have not served my country with greater ability, I have served it with a sincere devotion will accompany me as a source of unfailing gratification.

Happily, I shall carry with me from the public theater other sources, which those who love their country most will best appreciate. I shall behold it blessed with tranquillity and prosperity at home and with peace and respect abroad. I can indulge the proud reflection that the American people have reached in safety and success their 40th year as an independent nation; that for nearly an entire generation they have had experience of their present Constitution, the off-spring of their undisturbed deliberations and of their free choice; that they have found it to bear the trials of adverse as well as prosperous circumstances; to contain in its combination of the federate and elective principles a reconcilement of public strength with individual liberty, of national power for the defense of national rights with a security against wars of injustice, of ambition, and vain-glory in the fundamental provision which subjects all questions of war to the will of the nation itself, which is to pay its costs and feel its calamities. Nor is it less a peculiar felicity of this Constitution, so dear to us all, that it is found to be capable, without losing its vital energies, of expanding itself over a spacious territory with the increase and expansion of the community for whose benefit it was established.

And may I not be allowed to add to this gratifying spectacle that I shall read in the character of the American people, in their devotion to true liberty and to the Constitution which is its palladium, sure presages that the destined career of my country will exhibit a Government pursuing the public good as its sole object, and regulating its means by the great principles consecrated in its charter and by those moral principles to which they are so well allied; a Government which watches over the purity of elections, the freedom of speech and of the press, the trial by jury, and the equal interdict against encroachments and compacts between religion and the state; which maintains inviolably the maxims of public faith, the security of persons and property, and encourages in every authorized mode the general diffusion of knowledge which guarantees to public liberty its permanency and to those who possess the blessing the true enjoyment of it; a Government which avoids intrusions on the internal repose of other nations, and repels them from its own; which does justice to all nations with a readiness equal to the firmness with which it requires justice from them; and which, whilst it refines its domestic code from every ingredient not congenial with the precepts of an enlightened age and the sentiments of a virtuous people, seeks by appeals to reason and by its liberal examples to infuse into the law which governs the civilized world a spirit which may diminish the frequency or circumscribe the calamities of war, and meliorate the social and beneficent relations of peace; a Government, in a word, whose conduct within and without may bespeak the most noble of ambitions-- that of promoting peace on earth and good will to man.

These contemplations, sweetening the remnant of my days, will animate my prayers for the happiness of my beloved country, and a perpetuity of the institutions under which it is enjoyed.

***

Note from the Editor

Odin's Library Classics strives to bring you unedited and unabridged works of classical literature. As such this is the complete and unabridged version of the original English text. The English language has evolved since the writing and some of the words appear in their original form, or at least the most commonly used form at the time. This is done to protect the original intent of the author. If at any time you are unsure of the meaning of a word, please do your research on the etymology of that word. It is important to preserve the history of the English language.

Taylor Anderson

Made in the USA
Las Vegas, NV
26 May 2021